BETTA FISH
OWNER'S MANUAL

The Detailed Handbook Covering All the Information You Need to Manage Your Betta Fish, Which Includes Nutritional Management, Conversation, Health Housing Feeding And Much More.

BY
JOHN W. HENDERSON

COPYRIGHT © 2024 ALL RIGHT RESERVED

FIRST CHAPTER:

BETTA FISH OVERVIEW: A Comprehensive Overview of the Species

Siamese fighting fish, or betta fish, are among the most widely kept freshwater aquarium fish species in the world. For aficionados of all ages, their engaging habits, intricate fins, and striking colors make them ideal companions. We'll dive into the intriguing world of betta fish in this chapter, looking at their history, natural habitat, physical traits, and distinctive habits.

History and Origins:

Southeast Asian shallow waterways, especially those in Thailand, Cambodia, Vietnam, and Laos, are the native habitat of betta fish (Betta splendens). These areas' rice fields, floodplains, and sluggish streams are where they were first found. The alternate moniker "Siamese fighting fish" refers to bettas since they were originally bred for their aggression, which was used in the antiquated sport of Siamese fish fighting rather than for their vivid colors and long fins.

Dedicated enthusiasts have selectively bred betta fish throughout years, creating the vibrant and varied kinds we see today. With an emphasis on improving characteristics like color intensity, fin form, and general attractiveness, breeders have produced a diverse range of exquisite betta fish that are sold for aquariums.

Physical Features: Betta fish differ from other aquarium species due to a number of unique physical characteristics. Their bodies are usually elongated and exhibit a wide range of colors, including metallic tones, iridescent patterns, and shades of red, blue, green, and purple. Their intricate fins, which are shaped like a veil, crown, half-moon, delta, and double tail, are their most remarkable characteristics.

In contrast to female bettas, which are typically smaller and have shorter fins, male bettas, sometimes referred to as "cocks" or "fighters," have longer fins and brighter colors. The striking demonstration of hostility and territorial behavior, particularly against other males, is one of the most recognizable characteristics of male betta fish.

Natural Environment:

In their natural habitat, rice paddies, marshes, and meandering streams are home to betta fish that like warm, shallow waters rich in plant. Low oxygen levels and erratic water conditions are characteristics of these habitats, which have shaped bettas' special respiratory adaptations.

Betta fish are able to breathe air from the water's surface because to a unique organ known as the labyrinth organ. They can thrive in oxygen-starved settings where other fish species would perish because to their adaptability. Bettas are well ideal for confinement in aquariums since they can survive in very tiny amounts of water.

Separate Actions:

The intricate habits of betta fish are well known and are a reflection of their social connections and territorial character. Particularly male bettas are territorial and will fight tooth and nail to keep others out of their domain, particularly other male bettas. Alongside this aggressive posturing, raising gill covers, and flaring fins, there are stunning territorial displays.

During the mating season, bettas display fascinating courting behaviors in addition to their territorial character. Using the bubbles that come out of their mouths, male betta fish will construct bubble nests at the surface of the water. The male will lure the female to the bubble nest, where spawning takes place, after he has selected a suitable match. The male is in charge of protecting the eggs and fry until they hatch after spawning.

Result:

To provide betta fish the best care and enrichment possible while they are in captivity, one must have a thorough understanding of their history, appearance, natural environment, and distinctive habits. Aquarium hobbyists may design conditions that mirror the natural habitat of bettas and enhance their general health and well-being by understanding their behavioral features and evolutionary adaptations. We'll look at how to build up the ideal betta fish tank, keep the water clean, and give these fascinating fish the right food and attention in the next chapters.

CHAPTER 2:

BETTA FISH TANK CONFIGURATION: Dimensions, Furnishings, and Design

The first step in giving your aquatic pet a cozy and stimulating home is setting up a betta fish tank. The fundamentals of setting up the perfect betta fish habitat—tank size, equipment choice, water conditions, and décor options—will be covered in detail in this chapter.

Size of Tank:

The health and happiness of betta fish are greatly influenced by the size of the tank. Although bettas are often housed in little bowls or containers, bigger tanks with enough of swimming room are really better for them. For a single betta fish, a minimum tank size of 5 gallons (19 liters) is advised, however bigger tanks provide even better conditions. Bigger aquariums provide more consistent water quality, more efficient waste diversion, and more fish mobility.

Selection of Equipment:

A healthy aquarium ecology depends on selecting the appropriate equipment. Here are a few essential items of gear to think about:

1. System of Filtration: For the water in an aquarium to remain pure and free of dangerous contaminants, a dependable filter is required. Soft filtration systems with variable flow rates are recommended for betta fish tanks in order to reduce water currents, which might stress out the fish because of their fragile fins.

2. Warmer: Because they are tropical fish, betta fish need warm water, namely 78–82°F (25–28°C). It is important to have a submersible aquarium heater with an integrated thermostat in order to maintain consistent water temperatures within this range.

3. Thermometer: Invest in a high-quality aquarium thermometer to correctly monitor the water's temperature. To make sure the temperature stays within the ideal range for bettas, place the thermometer in a conspicuous spot within the tank.

4. Substrate: Pick a substrate that is both easily cleaned and safe for betta fish. Sand, fine gravel, or substrate materials safe for aquariums are good choices. Steer clear of abrasive or sharp surfaces that might harm your betta's fragile fins.

5. Illumination: Even while betta fish don't need special illumination, having a soft source of lighting in the aquarium may improve its visual appeal and, if wanted, encourage the development of live plants.

Water Specifications:

Betta fish health and welfare depend on maintaining the right water conditions. Key parameters to keep an eye on are as follows:

1. Climatic temperature: As was previously indicated, bettas like warm water, 78–82°F (25–28°C). Variations that fall outside of this range may cause stress to the fish and weaken their defenses.

2. pH Level: Water with a pH range of 6.5–7.5 is preferred by betta fish as being somewhat acidic as opposed to neutral. Maintaining the pH within the ideal range may be ensured by routinely checking the water using an aquarium pH test kit that is dependable.

3. Levels of Ammonia, Nitrite, and Nitrate: The nitrogen cycle in aquariums produces ammonia, nitrite, and nitrate as byproducts, which may be hazardous to fish at high doses. To maintain ideal water quality, use a high-quality aquarium test kit to periodically check these parameters and make partial water changes as necessary.

4. Intenseness: Although betta fish can tolerate a broad variety of water hardness levels, they are most comfortable in water that is mildly to moderately soft. Aim for 3–8 dKH for carbonate hardness and 5–15 dGH for general hardness.

Options for Decorating:

In addition to adding to the betta fish tank's aesthetic appeal, decorating it gives the fish hiding places and enrichment. Consider the following decorative options:

1. Living flora: In addition to improving the water quality of the aquarium by absorbing nitrates, adding live plants gives betta fish a feeling of security and natural hiding spots. Select water plants that need little maintenance, such Java fern, Anubias, Amazon sword, and Java moss.

2. Hardscape: Use naturally occurring hardscape components like driftwood, boulders, and caverns to provide betta fish hiding places and borders for their territories. Make sure the hardscape materials don't leak dangerous elements into the water and are safe for aquariums.

3. Artifice Ornaments: Artificial decorations like silk plants, porcelain ornaments, and PVC pipes may also provide visual interest and hiding spots to the tank if real plants aren't a possibility. Steer clear of ornaments that might harm your betta fish, such as those with sharp edges or rough surfaces.

4. Substrate Accents: Decorative substrate accents, including colorful gravel, sand, or natural stones, may improve the tank's visual appeal. Just be sure to completely clean the substrate to get rid of any dust or dirt before putting it to the tank.

Result:

It's important to carefully consider tank size, equipment choice, water conditions, and decoration choices while setting up the ideal betta fish aquarium. You may establish a flourishing home for your betta fish by giving them access to a large, well-equipped tank with consistent water conditions and plenty of possibilities for enrichment. For the best possible care and pleasure, we'll go over how to feed your betta fish, maintain water quality, and comprehend their distinct habits in the next chapters.

Chapter 3: Water Quality Management: Preserving Environmental Health

For betta fish to be healthy and happy, water quality is essential. We'll go into the significance of managing water quality in the betta fish tank in this chapter, including the nitrogen cycle, water testing, regular maintenance, and typical problems with water quality.

The Cycle of Nitrogen:
A stable and healthy aquarium ecology depends on an understanding of the nitrogen cycle. A naturally occurring biological process known as the nitrogen cycle transforms hazardous ammonia—which is created by leftover food, fish waste, and decomposing organic matter—into less dangerous substances called nitrite and nitrate.

1. **Ammonia:** Ammonia is a very harmful gas released into the water by fish waste and uneaten food. If left uncontrolled, it may cause stress, disease, and even death.

2. **Nitrite:** A process known as nitrification turns ammonia into nitrite, thanks to beneficial bacteria called Nitrosomonas. Even while nitrite is not as harmful as ammonia, high concentrations may still damage fish by reducing their ability to absorb oxygen.

3. **Sulfur:** Nitrobacter, a different class of helpful bacteria, further transforms nitrite into nitrate, which, in small amounts, is comparatively non-toxic to fish. Regular water changes remove nitrate from the aquarium, and

living plants may absorb it and use it as a source of nutrition.

A steady nitrogen cycle must be established and maintained to avoid surges in ammonia and nitrite, which may stress or damage betta fish. In order to stimulate the development of good bacteria, cycling a new aquarium usually requires the introduction of an ammonia source, such as fish food or pure ammonia, and takes 4-6 weeks.

Testing for Water:
In order to keep an eye on important water parameters and spot any problems before they become worse, regular water testing is necessary. The following are the main variables to look for along with the suggested thresholds:

1. **NH3/NH4+ ammonia:** Ammonia levels should ideally be negligible or almost nonexistent since fish may get stressed or harmed by measurable amounts. For easy testing, ammonia test kits are offered in liquid or test strip form.

2. **NO2-Nitrite**: Moreover, nitrite levels have to be negligible or almost absent since high concentrations might harm fish health. During the cycling phase, nitrite test kits should be utilized in addition to ammonia testing because they are easily accessible.

3. **NO3-Nitrate:** In order to avoid excessive algal development and preserve water quality, nitrate levels should be maintained at 20–40 ppm (parts per million). The best approach to

regulate the amount of nitrate in the aquarium is to do regular partial water changes.

4. **pH Level:** It is important that the water's pH stays steady within the ideal range of 6.5 to 7.5 for betta fish. Fish that experience abrupt pH changes may become stressed and have compromised immune systems.

5. **Climatic temperature:** Keep an eye on the water's temperature using a trustworthy aquarium thermometer to make sure it stays within the ideal range of 78–82°F (25–28°C) for betta fish.

Upkeep Schedules:
Creating a regular maintenance schedule is essential to maintaining the cleanliness and health of the betta fish tank. The following are

some crucial upkeep duties that should be completed every week or every two weeks:

1. Partial Water Alterations: Frequent partial water changes aid in clearing the aquarium of dissolved contaminants, extra nutrients, and accumulated waste. For best water quality, try to replace 20–30% of the water volume per week or as required.

2. **Gravel Vacuuming:** During water changes, use a gravel vacuum or siphon to clean the substrate and get rid of any leftover food, debris, and fish waste from the bottom of the tank.

3. **Maintenance of Filters:** To keep effective filtration going and avoid obstructions, clean or replace the filter material as required. To keep

beneficial bacteria colonies intact, rinse biological medium in dechlorinated water.

Cleaning Glass: Utilize a sponge or algae scraper designed for aquarium use to remove any accumulated algae from the tank's glass walls. Maintaining appearance and visibility requires regular cleaning.

5. **Taking Care of Plants:** During water changes, remove any algae-covered leaves and cut any dead or decaying plant materials if your aquarium has live plants. Make sure plants have enough light and nutrition to develop healthily.

Fixing Problems with Water Quality:
Sometimes there will be problems with the quality of the water even with your best efforts.

The following list of typical issues along with possible causes is

1. **Overcast Water:** Bacterial blooms, insufficient filtration, and overfeeding may all cause cloudy water. To determine the root cause, do a water test and modify feeding and filtration as necessary.

2. **Algae Growth:** Conditions with plenty of light and nutrients are ideal for algae growth. Reduce feeding, modify illumination duration, and do routine water changes to manage the development of algae. As an additional natural algae management method, think about adding fish or invertebrates that consume algae.

3. **Spikes of Ammonia or Nitrite:** An imbalance in the nitrogen cycle is indicated by

elevated levels of nitrite or ammonia. To keep fish from being stressed or harmed, increase water changes and keep a careful eye on the water's parameters. Steer clear of overfeeding and overcrowding, since both may cause surges in ammonia.

4. **pH Fluctuations:** Fish may get stressed and biological processes may be disturbed by abrupt pH shifts. Make sure the aquarium is correctly cycled, and keep the water steady by testing it and gradually changing the pH as needed.

Result:

Regular maintenance schedules and careful water quality control are necessary to keep betta fish in a healthy habitat. You can provide your betta fish with a healthy, stable, and clean environment by doing frequent water tests, knowing the nitrogen cycle, doing regular maintenance, and solving common problems. We'll go over feeding recommendations, betta fish health care, and ways to improve your betta fish's quality of life in the next chapters.

Part 4: Feeding Your Betta: Nutrition and Dietary Recommendations

For the sake of your betta fish's development, health, and general wellbeing, you must provide them a diet rich in nutrients and balance. This chapter will go over the nutritional needs of betta fish, appropriate foods to give them, feeding schedules, and typical feeding errors to watch out for.

Nutritional Guidelines:

Because betta fish are omnivores, they eat a variety of foods that include both plant and animal protein. Small insects, insect larvae, zooplankton, and plant materials found in their native environment are the main foods that bettas eat in the wild. It's crucial to provide them a wide variety of nutrient-dense meals in order to mimic their natural diet in captivity.

Serum: A meal rich in protein is essential for the growth, development of muscles, and general health of betta fish. Seek for fish meals designed especially for bettas, including fish meal, shrimp meal, or bug larvae, that have a high proportion of high-quality proteins.

Plant Substance: Even though their food is mostly carnivorous, bettas gain by include plant stuff in their diet. Vitamins, minerals, and fiber from plant-based diets are vital for healthy digestion and general well-being. On rare occasions, give your betta blanched veggies like spinach, zucchini, or peas as rewards.

Food Sources:

For betta fish, a variety of food kinds are available, each with special advantages and nutritional profiles. Here are a few typical eating choices to think about:

1. **Small Pellets:** Betta fish pellets are a handy, well-balanced feeding choice that provide vital nutrients in a small package. To guarantee bettas get the best nourishment possible, look for premium pellets made

especially for them. To avoid choking or overeating, choose a pellet size that corresponds to the size of your betta's mouth.

2. *Flakes:** Another well-liked meal choice that is convenient and gives diversity is betta fish flakes. Flakes are a good source of vitamins, lipids, and proteins for betta fish. But if not eaten right after, flakes may be messy and might worsen the quality of the water.

3. **Freeze-Dried or Frozen Foods:** Foods like bloodworms, brine shrimp, daphnia, and mosquito larvae that are frozen or freeze-dried are great choices for giving betta fish a varied and organic diet. These feeds replicate the live items that bettas eat in the wild and are high in protein. To avoid gastrointestinal problems,

make sure frozen meals are thawed before serving.

4. Living Foods: For betta fish, live meals like bloodworms, daphnia, and brine shrimp are very nourishing and stimulating. Live meals, however, should be carefully procured and quarantined to prevent the introduction of viruses and parasites into the aquarium. Use living foods as a complement to a balanced diet or as occasional pleasures.

Timetable of Feeding:
For optimum health and to avoid overfeeding or underfeeding, a consistent feeding plan must be established. The following are some recommendations for betta fish food:

1. **Recurrence:** Adult betta fish should be fed 1-2 times a day in little pieces that they can finish in two to three minutes. Refrain from overfeeding since this may result in obesity, digestive problems, and poor water quality.

2. **Coherence:** Maintain a regular feeding plan to keep your betta's metabolism under control and avoid stomach problems. Feed your betta at consistent times every day to create a habit that it can look forward to.

3. **Difference:** Provide a diverse range of food items to guarantee your betta has a well-rounded and nourishing diet. For diversity and enrichment, alternate between pellets, flakes, freeze-dried or frozen feeds, and live foods.

4. **Note:** To determine your betta fish's nutritional requirements and modify the quantity of food you give them, observe their behavior and hunger on a regular basis. Any changes in appetite, weight, or degree of exercise should be noted as they may point to underlying medical conditions.

Tips for Feeding and Errors to Avoid:
Here are some more feeding guidelines and typical blunders to stay away from in order to guarantee that your betta fish get the best nutrition possible and stay healthy:

1. Steer clear of overfeeding: Overfeeding is a typical error that may result in digestive difficulties, obesity, and poor water quality. To avoid overfeeding, provide modest, frequent

meals and take away any food that remains uneaten after feeding.

2. **Provide Appropriate Portions:** Give your betta food in manageable serving sizes that they may finish in a matter of minutes. Keep in mind that throwing a lot of food into the tank will pollute the water and produce a lot of trash.

3. **Quality Over Quantity:** Rather of offering generic fish meals, concentrate on offering premium foods that are especially made for betta fish. High-quality meals are lower in potential to contaminate water and include vital nutrients.

4. Keep an eye on the water quality: Food that has not been consumed may break down and cause water contamination and ammonia

increases. After feeding, be sure to remove any uneaten food to keep the aquarium's water quality at its best.

5. Steer clear of feeding fingers: Even though betta fish might be anxious to eat, don't hand feed them to avoid unintentional bites or injury. To provide food securely and without running the danger of harm, use feeding instruments like tweezers or a feeding ring.

Result:

It's essential for your betta fish's development, health, and general wellbeing to provide them a good, well-balanced food. You can give your betta fish the best nutrition possible and make sure they flourish in captivity by learning about their nutritional needs, providing a range of meals, setting up a regular feeding plan, and avoiding common feeding errors. For a thorough introduction to betta fish ownership, we'll cover topics like as behavior, tank companions, health care, and breeding advice in the next chapters.

Recognizing Betta Behavior: Indications of Stress and Illness

It's crucial to comprehend betta fish behavior in order to provide your aquatic pets the proper care and to guarantee their wellbeing. We'll look at a variety of betta fish behaviors in this chapter, including as aggressiveness, stress, courting, and health indicators.

Typical Conduct:

Betta fish are renowned for having colorful personalities and distinctive habits. Knowing their typical behavior patterns may help you spot any variations that could point to underlying medical conditions or stressful environmental factors. The following are common actions shown by well-groomed betta fish:

1. Intense Swimming: In good health, betta fish move about actively, investigating their surroundings and going about their daily lives doing things like hunting, foraging, and interacting with decorations in their tanks.

2. **Analysis:** Betta fish are inquisitive animals who want to investigate their environment. They may explore the plants, caverns, and other tank ornaments, periodically darting around or excitedly flaring their fins.

3. **Surfacing:** Male bettas will naturally flare in reaction to perceived threats or territorial conflicts. Bettas flaring look bigger and more menacing by spreading their fins and gill coverings. Fish may flare in reaction to other fish, reflections, or even a mirror image of themselves.

4. **Slumber:** Bettas need to relax sometimes to save their energy and keep their health at its best, much like other fish. A healthy betta may take a nap in the shadows, amid plants, or at the bottom of the tank.

5. **Feeding Response:** Betta fish have a strong need to eat, and when food is presented, they will rush to the water's surface. In advance of feeding time, they could engage in begging

behaviors including "dancing" at the water's surface or pleading at the front of the tank.

Healthy Signs:

It's critical to identify the telltale indicators of a healthy betta fish in order to assess its general health and make sure its demands are being satisfied. The following are some signs of a betta fish in good health:

1. **Bright Colors:** Healthy betta fish show no symptoms of fading or dullness, but rather brilliant colors and iridescent patterns. Environmental variables, food, and heredity may all affect how intense a color is.

2. Swimming with Movement: Healthy betta fish are energetic and vigilant, swimming the tank

with assurance and curiously investigating their environment.

3. Observe with Clear Eyes: A healthy betta fish should have bright, clear eyes that aren't cloudy or discolored. Prominent or cloudy eyes may be a sign of a more serious health problem.

4. **Open Fins:** Fully open fins and erect gill covers are signs of excellent general health and energy in healthy betta fish. Fins that are closed or clamped might indicate stress or disease.

5. **Nutritious Taste:** A powerful appetite and enthusiastic consumption of food at feeding times characterize a healthy betta fish. When food is presented, they might show joy and enthusiasm, eagerly seeking out and gorging on their meals.

Stress Indicators:

Stress may have a detrimental effect on the health and behavior of betta fish, which can result in a compromised immune system, increased illness susceptibility, and a shorter life span. Early stress sign detection enables you to address underlying problems and provide the proper therapy. These are a few typical indicators of stress in betta fish:

1. **Lethargy:** Stressed-out betta fish tend to become sedentary and inactive, spending more time hiding amid decorations at the bottom of the tank or resting.

2. Diminished Colors: Stress may make betta fish lose their vivid colors and iridescence, making them pale or fade in color. Colors that

seem dull or washed out might be signs of underlying stresses like aggressive tankmates or poor water quality.

3. **Fin Clamping:** Stressed-out betta fish may fold or compress their fins firmly against their body. Clamped fins may indicate pain, nervousness, or disease.

4. **Decrease in Hunger:** The betta fish may reject food or eat less than normal while under stress, which might reduce their appetite. Abrupt appetite loss might be a sign of underlying health problems or stresses that need to be addressed.

5. **Erratic Behavior:** Stressed-out betta fish could act strangely or erratically, scuttling about the tank, rubbing themselves against objects

repeatedly, or gasping for breath at the surface of the water. These actions may be a sign of pain or anguish.

treating Stressors: Restoring the health and wellbeing of your betta fish requires identifying and treating the root causes of stress. The following actions may help reduce stress in your betta fish:

1. Preserve Water Quality: For betta fish, poor water quality is a frequent source of stress. Make sure the water parameters in the aquarium are within the ideal range for betta fish and that the tank is cycled correctly. To avoid stress-related problems, do routine water changes and keep an eye on the levels of ammonia, nitrite, nitrate, pH, and temperature.

2. **Provide Enrichment:** Environments with plenty of excitement and enrichment are ideal for betta fish. Add real plants, caverns, and hiding places to the tank to provide a sense of security and to encourage natural behavior. Tank mates and decorations should not be crammed inside the tank, since this may cause territorial conflicts and tension.

3. Reducing disturbances: Stress-inducing vibrations, loud sounds, and abrupt movements may all be felt by betta fish. A peaceful spot away from busy streets is best for the aquarium, and you should try to avoid tapping the glass or moving the tank abruptly.

4. **Watch Your Tank Partners:** Territorial conflicts and injuries may arise from aggressive or incompatible tank mates, which can stress out

betta fish. To guarantee a harmonious cohabitation, choose your tank mates wisely and keep an eye on their interactions.

5. Give Adequate Nutrition: Retaining the health and stress tolerance of betta fish requires a diet rich in nutrients and balance. Provide an assortment of superior meals and steer clear of overindulging or underfeeding in order to avert stomach problems and inadequate nutrients.

Result:

It's essential to comprehend betta fish behavior in order to spot health and stress indicators and provide the proper treatment. You may assess your betta fish's general health, deal with any possible stresses, and provide a wholesome, stimulating habitat that encourages their natural habits by routinely studying their activity. We'll look at common health problems, tank mates for betta fish, and breeding advice for betta fish aficionados in the next chapters.

Tank Compatibility and Community Tank Options for Betta Fish: Chapter 6

Choosing the right tank mates for your betta fish can improve the dynamics of your aquarium and provide your fish companionship and enrichment. This chapter will cover community tank alternatives, compatibility concepts, and how to introduce tank mates to your betta fish environment.

Consistency Principles:

It's important to take compatibility into account when selecting tank mates for your betta fish, taking into account factors like temperament, size, and environmental needs. Even though betta fish are notorious for being aggressive against other males and fish with long, flowing fins, given the correct circumstances, they may live in harmony with other species. The following elements should be taken into account while choosing tank mates for your betta fish:

1. **Climatic Conditions:** Select companions for your betta fish that are calm or non-aggressive so they won't agitate or disturb them. Steer clear of animals that have a reputation for biting fins or acting aggressively in the aquarium since this may cause stress and conflict.

2. **Depth:** Choose tank mates that are at least as big as your betta fish to reduce the possibility of predators or aggressive behavior. Selecting companions for your betta fish that are much smaller than them is not a good idea since they can be seen as possible food and harassed.

3. **Level of Swimming:** When choosing species for your community tank, take into account the habitat and preferred swimming level of possible tank mates. Select fish species that live at various depths in the water column, such as those that are bottom, mid-water, and surface-dwelling, to lessen competition for food and space.

4. **Water Specifications:** Make sure the water parameters of the tank mates you choose, such as temperature, pH, hardness, and oxygen

levels, meet your betta fish's needs. Fish from different species should not be paired together since this might cause stress and other health problems for the fish.

5. Examining Compatibility: Gradually introduce possible tank mates to your betta fish and keep a careful eye on their interactions to see whether they get along. If hostility or stress become a problem, be ready to rehome or remove unsuitable tank mates.

* Options for Community Tanks:**
Because they are territorial fish, bettas are often kept as solitary pets, but in a well-designed community tank, they may live in harmony with other fish species. The following list of compatible tank mates for betta fish has a high compatibility rate:

1. **Small Schooling Fish:** Betta fish may have a great time in a tank with peaceful schooling fish like neon tetras, harlequin rasboras, ember tetras, and celestial pearl danios. Because these species are swift, tiny, and non-aggressive, bettas are less prone to become hostile against them.

2. **Bottom-Dwelling Species:** Betta fish may live in harmony with bottom-dwelling species like kuhli loaches, corydoras catfish, and tiny kinds of plecos. These fish live in the lowest sections of the tank and scavenge food leftovers and debris to keep the substrate clean.

3. **Shrimp and Snails:** Betta fish may have colorful and fascinating tank companions in the form of dwarf shrimp species including cherry

shrimp, amano shrimp, and ghost shrimp. In a similar vein, calm snail species like mystery and nerite snails may assist in clearing algae off tank walls and ornaments.

4. **Tiny Non-Aggressive Animals:** In bigger community tanks with plenty of room and hiding places, other tiny, non-aggressive species like platies, guppies, endlers, and mollies could get along well with betta fish. Male guppies should not be kept alongside betta fish since the male bettas may get aggressive because to their vivid colors and long fins.

5. Invertebrate species: Calm invertebrates like tiny crabs, freshwater shrimp, and snails may be interesting tank companions for betta fish. It is important to consider the size and behavior of the invertebrates you choose since betta fish may

see bigger or more aggressive species as possible food.

Announcing Your Tank Companion

To reduce stress and any disputes, it's important to move cautiously when adding new tank mates to your betta fish environment. Here are some pointers for introducing your betta fish to new tankmates:

1. **Quarantine New Fish:** Before adding new fish to your betta fish environment, quarantine them for at least two weeks in a separate tank to look for symptoms of sickness or disease. This lessens the chance of diseased fish entering your aquarium and helps stop the spread of infections.

2. **Offer Hiding Spots:** Make sure the aquarium has enough hiding places and visible obstacles for the betta fish as well as the newcomers before adding more tank mates. This enables fish to mark their territories and, in an emergency, withdraw to safe areas.

3. **Observed Exchanges:** Gradually add additional tankmates to the aquarium, putting the least aggressive species in there initially. Keep a watchful eye out for any indications of hostility, tension, or compatibility problems in their encounters. If required, be ready to rehome or remove unsuitable tank mates.

4. **Serve Fish Alone:** Feeding your betta fish and tank mates separately may help to lessen hostility at feeding time and reduce competition for food. Use target feeding or

feeding rings to make sure every fish has enough food without running the danger of a fight.

5. **Note Conduct:** During the introduction phase, pay special attention to how the betta fish and the new tankmates behave. To keep the aquarium peaceful, keep an eye out for any indications of tension, hostility, or compatibility. Then, be ready to step in and make any necessary modifications or interventions.

Result:

Choosing the right tank mates for your betta fish can improve the dynamics of your aquarium and provide your fish companionship and enrichment. It is possible to design a peaceful community tank that meets the requirements of your betta fish as well as those of their tankmates by taking into account variables like temperament, size, swimming ability, and environmental requirements. The care of betta fish, typical health problems, and breeding advice for betta fish fans will all be covered in the next chapters.

Chapter 7: Health Care for Betta Fish: Avoidance, Identifying, and Handling of Common Problems

Your betta fish's length and quality of life depend on you taking care of their health and wellbeing. This chapter will cover methods for keeping your betta fish healthy and vibrant, including identifying symptoms of disease, treating them appropriately, and avoiding common health problems.

Avoidance Care:

Maintaining the health and disease-resilience of your betta fish depends heavily on preventive care. You may reduce the risk of health problems and enhance general wellbeing by using proper husbandry techniques and preserving ideal water quality. The following are some betta fish preventative care techniques:

1. **Correct Tank Setup:** Begin by giving your betta fish a suitable habitat, which should include a large enough tank, a sufficient filtration system, and the right water parameters. Make that the tank has been cycled correctly and is clear of any poisons, contaminants, or dangerous materials.

2. **Timely Water Replacements:** To keep the aquarium's water quality at its best and get rid of dissolved contaminants, extra nutrients, and accumulated trash, do partial water changes on a regular basis. For the purpose of controlling the levels of ammonia, nitrite, and nitrate, try to replace 20–30% of the water volume once a week or as required.

3. Optimal Nutrition: Provide a well-rounded and nourishing diet for your betta fish by giving it premium store-bought meals, live foods, and infrequent treats. Steer clear of both underfeeding and overfeeding, since both may result in nutritional deficiencies, obesity, and digestive problems.

4. **Environmental Enrichment:** Decorate the tank with live plants, caverns, hiding places, and

tank mates (if suitable) to give your betta fish plenty of excitement and enrichment. Enrichment encourages natural behaviors and mental stimulation while lowering stress, boredom, and aggressive tendencies.

5. **Consistent Monitoring:** Keep a watchful eye out for any changes in your betta fish's appearance, temperament, appetite, or level of activity. Frequent observation enables you to identify any health problems early on and take quick action to stop them from becoming worse.

Identifying Common Health Concerns:

Even with the finest of care, betta fish may sometimes still have health problems. Knowing the telltale signs and symptoms of common health issues enables you to respond appropriately and provide treatment on time. The following are some typical health problems betta fish may experience:

1. **Contagious Diseases:** Fuzzy or cottony growths on the fish's body, fins, or gills are indicative of fungal illnesses such fin rot or cotton wool disease (Columnaris). Frayed or ragged fins, tiredness, and appetite loss are possible additional symptoms.

2. **Infections by Bacteria:** Redness, inflammation, swelling, bloating, and elevated scales are some of the signs that may be caused by bacterial infections, such as bacterial fin rot or bacterial dropsy. Fish may also show signs of weakness, appetite loss, and labored respiration.

3. **Infections with Pathogens:** Microscopic parasites that adhere to the fish's skin, gills, or fins are the source of parasitic illnesses, including ich (white spot disease), velvet disease, and flukes. White patches, fatigue, clawing at objects, and fast breathing are possible symptoms.

4. Disorders of the Swim Bladder:** Problems with buoyancy brought on by swim bladder diseases might manifest as symptoms like floating, sinking, or irregular swimming. Fish may also become lethargic, lose their appetite, and have trouble staying balanced.

5. **Dropsy:** A dangerous ailment called dropsy is characterized by bloating, swelling, and fluid retention in the fish's body cavity. Raised scales, bulging eyes, fatigue, appetite

loss, and breathing difficulties are possible additional symptoms.

Management of Typical Health Concerns:

Treating common health problems as soon as possible is crucial to keeping them from becoming worse. Treatment choices may differ based on the kind and severity of the disease. The following are some broad approaches to treating common health problems in betta fish:

1. **Medication:** Use the right drugs, such as antibiotics, antifungals, or antiparasitics, to treat bacterial, fungal, or parasite illnesses. To guarantee that the infections are effectively eradicated, attentively follow the manufacturer's instructions and dosage guidelines and finish the whole course of therapy.

2. **Water Alteredries:** To keep the water at its ideal quality and lessen the strain on the fish's immune system, replace the water often. Water that is pure and oxygenated aids in the healing and recuperation process.

3. **Quarantine:** To stop the spread of illness and provide targeted care, isolate sick or wounded fish in a different quarantine tank. To aid with the fish's recuperation, quarantine tanks need to have the proper filtration, heating, and aeration systems.

4. **Temperature Adjustment:** To provide your betta fish the best possible healing environment, adjust the water's temperature as necessary. Lower temperatures may impede the course of certain illnesses, while higher

temperatures can speed up the immune system and metabolism.

5. **Reduction of Stress:** Reduce the amount of stress the fish experience by creating a calm, low-stress environment with enough hiding places and visible obstacles. Keep your fish away from stressful situations that might weaken their immune systems, such as crowded tanks, hostile tankmates, and abrupt changes in the water's characteristics.

Result:

To keep your betta fish healthy and happy, you must be proactive in providing preventative care, recognize common health problems early, and take the right measures to therapy when it's required. Your betta fish will flourish in captivity if you follow proper husbandry procedures, keep the water at its ideal level, feed them a balanced food, and keep a careful eye out for any symptoms of disease or distress. For betta fish aficionados who want to take their passion to the next level, we'll go over advanced care procedures, tank layout suggestions, and breeding advice in the next chapters.

Chapter 8: Strategies, Methods, and Factors to Take Into Account

For aquarium hobbyists, breeding betta fish may be a gratifying and exciting experience. This chapter delves into the realm of betta fish breeding, examining the steps involved, as well as helpful hints, methods, and crucial factors to take into account for fruitful reproduction.

A Brief Overview of Betta Fish Breeding

In order to breed betta fish, a male and female must be paired together in a regulated setting with ideal circumstances for spawning, incubating eggs, and raising fry. Even though raising betta fish may be difficult and requires careful planning and attention to detail, it can also be a very fulfilling pastime for enthusiasts who want to learn more and help preserve different betta fish kinds.

Choosing Reproductive Stock:

The first stage in breeding betta fish is selecting appropriate breeding stock. To produce robust, healthy offspring, it is important to choose healthy, high-quality fish with desired features. When choosing breeding stock, keep the following things in mind:

1. **Well-being and State:** Select betta fish that show no symptoms of disease, deformities, or genetic anomalies, and that are in excellent general health and condition. Seek for fish that have vivid hues, straight fins, and lively movements.

2. **Genetic variety:** To preserve genetic variety and reduce the likelihood of genetic abnormalities or health problems in the progeny, avoid inbreeding by choosing unrelated or genetically varied breeding pairings.

3. **Preferred Qualities:** Think about the ideal qualities you want to encourage in the progeny, including body form, color, finnage, and pattern. Selecting breeding stock with these qualities will make it more likely that the progeny will turn out well.

4. **Congruency:** To improve the chances of a successful spawning and fry survival, pair betta fish with similar temperaments and breeding habits. Refrain from producing violent or incompatible people who might hurt one other.

Installation for Breeding:

In order to initiate spawning behavior and provide a secure, favorable habitat for betta fish to reproduce, it is essential to provide an appropriate breeding environment. The following are essential elements of a breeding setup:

1. **Tank for Breeding:** To ensure that the breeding couple and their young have enough room, use a separate breeding tank or spawning tank that has a minimum volume of 5 to 10 gallons. Make sure the tank has a tight-fitting cover or lid to stop jumpers and keep the water parameters steady.

2. **Material:** A smooth, non-abrasive substrate, such fine gravel or sand, should be placed at the bottom of the breeding tank to provide a suitable surface for the deposition of eggs and shield the fragile eggs from harm.

3. **Hidden Locations:** Give the breeding couple plenty of places to hide and visible obstacles so they may mark their territories and flee to safety if necessary. To build hiding areas and spawning grounds, use PVC pipes, spawning mops, fake or real plants, and floating vegetation.

4. **Quality of Water:** To encourage spawning behavior and fry growth, keep the temperature, pH, hardness, and cleanliness of the water at ideal levels. To eliminate waste and preserve water purity, keep the water temperature between 78 and 82°F (25 and 28°C) and do frequent water changes.

Behavior of Spawning:

The male and female betta fish usually engage in a wooing ritual before reproducing. In order to attract the female and persuade her to spawn, the male betta constructs a bubble nest at the water's surface using air bubbles and saliva. The following are important features of betta fish spawning behavior:

1. **Building a Bubble Nest:** Using his mouth and fins, the male betta creates air bubbles at the water's surface to build a bubble nest. After that, he organizes the bubbles into a raft or mat that floats and protects the nest from outside interference.

2. **Displays of Courtship:** In order to get the female's attention, the male betta engages in courting activities such as flaring his fins, showcasing vivid colors, and engaging in

elaborate dances or motions around the nest location.

3. ** Fertilization of Eggs:** The female visits the male's nest when she is ready to spawn, and they have a brief courting dance. As the female releases the eggs into the nest, the male encircles her with his body and releases milk, or sperm, to fertilize them.

4. **Collection of Eggs:** Following spawning, the male takes the fertilized eggs and places them in his mouth, allowing them to stick to the surface of the bubble nest on the bottom. Before the male chases her away, the female could help gather and move eggs to the nest.

Fry Gathering:

Following spawning, the male betta takes charge of providing the best environment for the growth of the eggs and fry, as well as protecting the bubble nest. Here are a few crucial elements in raising fry:

1. **Maintenance of Bubble Nests:** The male betta keeps a careful eye on the bubble nest, fixing any broken bubbles and making sure the eggs stay floating within the framework of the nest. In order to give the eggs oxygen and stop fungus from growing, he would softly fan them with his fins.

2. **Incubation of Eggs:** In general, the fertilized eggs hatch in 24-48 hours, contingent upon environmental conditions and water temperature. After hatching, the fry are held to

the bubble nest by an adhesive gland until they are able to swim freely.

Step 3: **Free-Swimming** When the fry are able to swim freely, they depend on their yolk sacs for nourishment and may display unpredictable swimming patterns as they investigate their environment. During this crucial developmental period, the male betta keeps watch over the fry and tends to the bubble nest.

4. **Initial Meals:** The fry need regular feedings of powdered or live food, such as infusoria, microworms, or commercial fry feeds, until their yolk sacs are depleted. Move on to bigger feeds gradually as the fry develop and expand.

Result:

For aquarium aficionados, raising betta fish may be an exciting and fulfilling hobby that offers valuable insights into the natural habits and reproductive techniques of this intriguing species. You may improve the chances of successful reproduction and aid in the preservation of betta fish variations by choosing proper breeding stock, setting up an ideal breeding environment, watching spawning behavior, and giving the fry the care they need. We'll look at genetic factors, innovative breeding methods, and advice on growing healthy betta fry to maturity in the next chapters.

Chapter 9: Genetic Considerations and Advanced Breeding Methods for Betta Fish

For those who want to learn more about genetics and selective breeding, producing betta fish may be a complex and exciting project. This chapter will cover advanced breeding methods, genetic factors to take into account, and tactics to produce desired traits and features in betta fish.

Choice of Breeds:

A key concept in betta fish breeding is selective breeding, which pairs individuals with desired qualities on purpose to create offspring with comparable features. Breeders may maximize desired qualities and minimize unwanted ones by carefully selecting betta fish with certain colors, fin kinds, patterns, and other characteristics.

Comprehension of Genetics:

Successful betta fish breeding requires an understanding of fundamental genetics. Through the transfer of genetic information, betta fish acquire qualities from its parents like as color, finnage, pattern, and other characteristics. The following are important genetic ideas to think about:

1. **Genetic diversity:** A variety of phenotypic features, including color, fin type, and pattern, are produced by the extensive genetic diversity present in betta fish. Natural selection, artificial selection via selective

breeding, and genetic mutation are some of the forces that affect genetic variety.

2. Traits that Are Dominant and Recessive: Certain qualities in betta fish breeding might be dominant or recessive, which means that their expression varies based on their genetic inheritance. Recessive qualities can only be exhibited when both copies of the gene are present, while dominant features may be expressed in either or both of the gene's copies.

3. **Polygenic Traits:** A number of betta fish characteristics, including color intensity and finnage, are polygenic, which means that many genes interact to impact them. The continuous range of variation shown by polygenic characteristics makes them more difficult to anticipate and manage via selective breeding.

4. Genetic Conditions: Genetic problems or health difficulties in betta fish, such as spine deformities, swim bladder disorders, or decreased fertility, may be caused by certain genetic mutations or anomalies. Responsible breeding procedures should be used by breeders to reduce the likelihood of developing genetic problems.

Sophisticated Breeding Methods:

Breeders may more successfully modify genetic characteristics and accomplish particular breeding objectives thanks to advanced breeding procedures. Here are a few cutting-edge breeding methods often used in the production of betta fish:

1. **Line Breeding:** In order to reinforce desired features and fix them within a breeding line, line breeding entails breeding closely related individuals, such as siblings or parent-offspring pairs. Although line breeding may contribute to the preservation of genetic purity and consistency, it also lowers genetic variety over time and raises the danger of genetic illnesses.

2. *Outcrossing* By marrying individuals from unrelated or genetically distant lineages, outcrossing introduces genetic variety into a reproductive line. In addition to boosting hybrid vigor and introducing novel traits or features into the breeding population, outcrossing aids in the prevention of inbreeding depression.

3. **Inbreeding:** In order to concentrate good qualities and generate more predictable offspring, closely related individuals are bred together. Inbreeding raises the possibility of genetic flaws, health problems, and decreased fertility in the progeny, but it may also assist correct desirable features and produce uniformity within a breeding line.

4. **Selective Pairing:** Selective pairing is the process of carefully choosing breeding partners based on certain qualities, attributes, or interesting genetic markers. Breeders may increase desirable features and generate offspring with enhanced genetic quality and consistency by matching people with complimentary traits.

Genetic Points to Remember:

It's crucial to think about the genetic effects of every breeding choice made while raising betta fish and to work toward preserving genetic variety, health, and vitality in the breeding population. The following genetic factors should be taken into account:

1. Diversity in Genetics: Preserving genetic variation is essential to maintaining the general well-being and adaptability of the betta fish population. To minimize genetic stagnation and lower the danger of genetic illnesses, avoid excessive inbreeding and work to introduce fresh genetic material via outcrossing and selective matching.

2. **Medical Examination:** Perform health exams before to mating betta fish in order to find

any possible abnormalities, illnesses, or genetic problems that might impact the breeding couple or their progeny. To reduce the risk of genetic problems being passed on to subsequent generations, choose breeding stock that is in excellent general health, vibrant, and genetically intact.

3. **Genetic Testing:** To determine the genetic heritage and background of possible breeding stock, think about carrying out genetic testing or pedigree analysis. In order to accomplish certain breeding objectives, genetic testing may be used to identify carriers of recessive characteristics, forecast the phenotypes of children, and make well-informed breeding choices.

4. **Aims for Breeding:** Clearly state your aims and goals for breeding, including the intended qualities, traits, and genetic results. Create a breeding strategy or plan that details the actions required to accomplish your objectives and monitors the progress of your breeding program over time.

Result:

The intricate and fulfilling hobby of raising betta fish calls for a deep understanding of genetics, breeding practices, and genetic factors. Breeders may strive toward creating betta fish with desired qualities, attributes, and genetic integrity by using sophisticated breeding procedures, comprehending genetic concepts, and making well-informed breeding choices. The subsequent chapters will include advanced care methods for adult betta fish, tactics for sustaining productive breeding operations, and advice for rearing healthy betta fry.

Chapter 10: Caring, Nutrition, and Growth for a Healthy Betta Fry

The intriguing process of raising betta fish from egg to maturity calls for close consideration of their particular developmental requirements. We'll go over care procedures, dietary needs, development targets, and typical roadblocks in this chapter as we examine the process of rearing healthy betta fry.

Beta Fry's Introduction:

Breeding partners lay eggs that hatch into betta fry, sometimes referred to as baby bettas or frylings. As they grow and mature, betta fry go through many developmental phases. It may be a pleasant and difficult experience to raise betta fry; it takes commitment, tolerance, and a deep understanding of their requirements as they mature.

Management Methods:

Betta fry need the best care possible to ensure their survival, development, and well-being. The following are some essential care methods for growing wholesome betta fry:

1. **Quality of Water:** By doing routine water changes, keeping an eye on the water's parameters, and getting rid of debris or uneaten

food right away, you can keep the fry tank's water pure. Water that is clear and well-oxygenated encourages development and lowers the chance of illness.

2. **Lighting and Temperature:** Using a dependable aquarium heater, maintain the fry tank's temperature around 78–82°F (25–28°C). To mimic natural daylight cycles and encourage normal growth, use low-intensity aquarium lights to create a soft lighting environment.

3. **Dietary Guidelines:** To encourage their quick growth and development, feed betta fry high-quality live or powdered foods often in tiny meals. To guarantee a balanced diet, provide a range of meals, including microworms, recently hatched brine shrimp, infusoria, and commercial fry feeds.

4. **Set Up Tank:** To provide the fry a secure, stress-free environment, use a separate fry tank or breeding tank that has a sponge filter and a calm water flow. Provide hiding places, living plants, and floating vegetation to provide the fry with protection and a place to stay.

5. **Watching and Tracking:** Keep a tight eye out for any indications of disease, stress, or aberrant development in the fry. Keep an eye out for any changes in growth rate, appetite, or behavior, and take quick action if anything seems off.

Ingredients for Nutrition:

In order to sustain their fast growth and development throughout the early stages of life, betta fry have unique dietary needs. Betta fry must be fed a diverse and well-balanced diet in order for them to get the vital elements they need to flourish. For betta fry, keep in mind the following important nutritional factors:

1. **Protein-Rich Foods:** To promote tissue growth, muscular development, and general health, betta fry need a diet heavy in high-quality protein. Provide live or frozen meals to provide necessary amino acids and protein sources, such as microworms, recently hatched brine shrimp, and daphnia.

2. **Tiny Particle Dimensions:** Select items that are appropriate for the tiny mouths of betta fry by looking for small particle sizes. The best things to give betta fry are freshly hatched brine

shrimp, microworms, infusoria, and commercial fry meals designed for tiny fry.

3. **Dietary Additives:** To guarantee the fry has the best nutrition possible and avoid deficiencies, think about adding vitamin and mineral supplements to its diet. While vitamins and minerals may be added to commercial fry meals, homemade or live food diets may need supplementation.

4. **Feeding Frequency:** Because betta fry have tiny stomachs and quick metabolisms, they need to eat little, frequent meals all day long in order to get the nourishment they require. Small quantities of food should be given to betta fry four to six times a day in order to avoid overfeeding and preserve water quality.

5. Making the Switch to Solid Foods: Gradually introduce solid meals, such pellets, live foods, or finely crushed flakes, to betta fry as they grow and mature. When the fry go from larvae to juveniles, supply a range of items to promote acceptance and provide a balanced diet.

Milestones for Growth:

In the first several weeks of their lives, betta fry grow and develop quickly, going through many developmental phases before reaching maturity. The following significant developmental phases and growth benchmarks have been noted in betta fry:

1. **Stage of eggs:** When breeding partners lay eggs and attach them to the bottom of the bubble nest, betta fry set off on their voyage.

Depending on environmental conditions and water temperature, the eggs usually hatch in 24-48 hours.

2. **Atlantic Phase:** Following hatching, betta fry cling to the bubble nest with the help of an adhesive gland and feed on the yolk sacs. Fry develop very little and are comparatively sedentary at this time.

Step 3: **Free-Swimming** The fry start investigating their environment, looking for food, and acting more actively once they can swim freely. Fry may swim erratically at first, but as they get older, they will eventually learn to swim more steadily.

4. **Color Creation:** Betta fry develop and grow, and as they do, their coloring starts to

show. It becomes stronger and more distinct with time. Fry may have soft, pastel colors at first, but as they get older, bright colors and patterns will emerge.

5. **Fin Development:** As betta fries become larger, their dorsal, anal, and caudal fins start to lengthen and become more noticeable. Individual differences in fin growth may be attributed to a combination of environmental, dietary, and genetic variables.

Typical Difficulties:

Breeders may run across a number of difficulties and barriers while raising betta fry. In order to guarantee the wellbeing and longevity of betta fry, it is essential to comprehend and tackle these obstacles. The following are some typical difficulties that arise while caring for betta fry:

1. Low-quality water: It is essential to maintain ideal water quality for the growth and well-being of betta fry. Fry development problems, disease, and stress may all be caused by poor water quality. To maintain perfect water conditions, periodically check the parameters of the water and replace the water often.

2. **Congested areas:** In the fry tank, overcrowding may cause stress, hostility, and competition for food. To prevent violence and territorial behavior, give your fry plenty of room and hiding places. If crowding starts to become a problem, you may also want to try dividing your fry into smaller groups.

3. **Disease and Parasites:** In crowded or unhygienic environments, betta fry are particularly vulnerable to illnesses and parasites. Keep an eye out for symptoms of sickness, such as fatigue, lack of appetite, and strange behavior, and quickly place the afflicted fries under quarantine to stop the infection from spreading.

4. The Cannibal Society: In betta fry tanks, cannibalism is a frequent problem, especially when fry are kept in big groups. To discourage violence and cannibalistic behavior, provide fry plenty of hiding places and visible obstacles. If needed, divide the fry into smaller groups.

5. **Anomalies of Development:** Developmental anomalies or malformations, including as twisted spines, malformed fins, or spinal curvature, may be seen in certain betta

fry. These anomalies might be inherited or the consequence of external influences. If necessary, select afflicted animals to save them from suffering, and keep a keen eye out for any indications of aberrant growth in the fry.

Result:

It's important to pay close attention to the specific developmental demands, dietary needs, and environmental factors of betta fry in order to ensure their health. Breeders may encourage the growth and development of betta fry and add to the success of their breeding program by giving them the best possible care, diet, and supervision. The advanced care methods for adult betta fish, breeding colony maintenance advice, and breeding goal tactics will all be covered in the next chapters.

The Elements of Advanced Betta Fish Care: Chapter 11

The lifespan, vigor, and general quality of life of adult betta fish depend on their health and wellbeing being maintained. This chapter will cover advanced care methods and approaches, including as habitat enrichment, illness prevention, and behavioral enrichment, that are essential to giving adult betta fish the best possible care.

Enrichment of Habitat:

Improving the environment of adult betta fish is essential for encouraging their natural activities, lowering stress levels, and improving their general wellbeing. Consider the following cutting-edge habitat augmentation methods:

1. Living flora: In order to provide the aquarium natural filtration, oxygenation, and shelter, use living plants. Pick plants that are good for bettas, including water lettuce or duckweed, as well as floating plants like Anubias, Java fern, and Amazon sword. In addition to preserving water quality, live plants help provide betta fish a more lifelike habitat.

2. **Components of Hardscape:** Create hiding places, territorial borders, and visual appeal in the aquarium by adding hardscape components like driftwood, rocks, caverns, and decorations.

Place hardscape components to resemble natural environments and provide hiding places and possibilities for exploration.

3. **Types of Substance:** Try experimenting with various substrate materials, including aquasoil, sand, or fine gravel, to give the aquarium a variety of textures and eye-catching features. Select surfaces that are good for living plants and safe for betta fish. To encourage plant development, apply root tabs or liquid fertilizers.

4. **Tips for Landscaping:** Create aquarium layouts that are both aesthetically pleasing and ecologically varied by using aquascaping methods like the Dutch, nature, or biotope styles. Try a variety of layouts, plant combinations, and focal points to create a harmonious and visually appealing aquascape.

5. Aquarium Illumination: To encourage plant development, bring out the colors of the fish, and replicate natural sunshine cycles, use the right aquarium lighting. To establish the best possible lighting conditions for your betta fish and plants, use full-spectrum or LED lighting fixtures with adjustable color temperature and intensity settings.

Prevention of Diseases:

Maintaining the health and vigor of adult betta fish requires preventing sickness. Taking proactive steps to avoid sickness may reduce the likelihood of illness and maintain the health and well-being of your betta fish. The following are some cutting-edge methods of illness prevention to think about:

1. **Quarantine Protocol:** To stop the spread of parasites and illnesses, quarantine any additional fish, plants, or aquarium equipment before adding them to the main tank. Before moving the quarantined individuals to the main tank, keep a watchful eye out for any symptoms of disease and use a separate quarantine tank with its own filtration system.

2. **Managing Water Quality:** To promote betta fish health and immunological function, maintain ideal water quality parameters, such as temperature, pH, ammonia, nitrite, and nitrate levels. To get rid of trash and maintain constant water parameters, do routine substrate vacuuming, water changes, and filter maintenance.

3. **Sanitation Procedures:** To reduce the amount of organic waste, debris, and algae that accumulates in the aquarium, practice excellent hygiene and aquarium management. To avoid excessive waste buildup, refrain from overfeeding and clean the aquarium's glass, decorations, and filter media on a regular basis using aquarium-safe cleaning supplies.

4. **Quarantine Protocol:** To stop the spread of parasites and illnesses, quarantine any additional fish, plants, or aquarium equipment before adding them to the main tank. Before moving the quarantined individuals to the main tank, keep a watchful eye out for any symptoms of disease and use a separate quarantine tank with its own filtration system.

5. Cleaning Procedures: To reduce the amount of organic waste, debris, and algae that accumulates in the aquarium, practice excellent hygiene and aquarium management. To avoid excessive waste buildup, refrain from overfeeding and clean the aquarium's glass, decorations, and filter media on a regular basis using aquarium-safe cleaning supplies.

6. **Nutritional promote:** Give adult betta fish a well-balanced and nutrient-rich food to promote their general health, vigor, and immune system. To make sure that betta fish get the vital vitamins, minerals, and nutrition they need, provide a range of premium commercial diets, live foods, and infrequent treats.

Enrichment via Behavior:

Encouraging natural activities and offering mental stimulation chances are critical to the health of adult betta fish. Consider the following cutting-edge behavioral enrichment methods:

1. **Friends of the Tank:** Provide social interaction and enrichment to the betta fish environment by adding appropriate tank mates. Select calm species that get along well with betta fish; steer clear of territorial or aggressive fish that might agitate or upset them.

2. Interactive Playthings: Give betta fish interactive toys, puzzles, or floating things to study, play with, and explore. Ping pong balls, floating food rings, floating plants, and mirrors may all pique people's attention and promote instinctive activities like searching and exploring.

3. **Variety in Environment:** Occasionally rearrange the ornaments, add fresh plants or hiding places, or add interesting items or stimuli to the tank. Betta fish benefit from environmental enrichment by being less stressed, less bored, and more mentally stimulated.

4. **Meal Preparation Methods:** When feeding, use strategies like target feeding, slow-release feeders, or food puzzles to stimulate the mind and promote natural foraging habits. Use feeding rings or scatter food over the water's surface to entice betta fish to look for and catch their prey.

5. *Changes in the Environment:** Provide betta fish with a dynamic and exciting habitat by imitating natural environmental changes, such as

seasonal fluctuations, day-night cycles, or changes in water flow. Utilize air pumps, wavemakers, or programmable timers to replicate natural aquarium conditions.

Result:

Adult betta fish must have their health, energy, and general well-being maintained via the use of sophisticated care procedures and tactics. A vibrant and peaceful aquarium environment may be created by betta fish hobbyists by enhancing the ecosystem, avoiding illness, and encouraging natural behaviors in their cherished aquatic pets. We'll look at how to keep breeding colonies going strong, solve frequent problems, and improve your betta fish keeping abilities in the next chapters.

Part 12: Sustaining an Effective Betta Fish Breeding Colony

A betta fish breeding colony must be established and successfully maintained, which calls for meticulous preparation, oversight, and attention to detail. The essential elements of a healthy betta fish breeding colony will be discussed in this chapter, along with breeding partner selection, colony management strategies, genetic variety, and long-term sustainability.

Choosing a Breeding Pair:

The cornerstone of a successful betta fish breeding colony is the selection of compatible breeding couples. To generate kids with the best possible genetic quality and vitality, breeding pairings should have desirable features, genetic variety, and general well-being. When choosing breeding couples, keep the following things in mind:

1. Diversity in Genetics: To preserve genetic variety within the breeding colony and reduce the likelihood of genetic illnesses or deformities, choose breeding couples with a range of genetic origins. To provide fresh genetic material to the breeding population, choose people that are genetically distant from each other or unrelated. Steer clear of severe inbreeding.

2. **Preferred Qualities:** Choose breeding couples with obvious patterns, distinct finnage, bright colors, and well-proportioned bodies as

your selections. Selecting couples that correspond with your intended results requires careful consideration of your breeding program's breeding goals and objectives.

3. **Well-being and State:** Make that breeding couples are free from symptoms of disease, deformities, or genetic anomalies, and that they are in excellent general health and condition. To evaluate possible breeding pairings, do physical examinations, watch behavior, and perform health exams.

4. **Congruency:** To improve the chances of a successful spawning and fry survival, pair betta fish with similar temperaments, habits, and physical attributes. During the breeding process, stay away from coupling aggressive or

incompatible individuals who might hurt one other or their progeny.

Methods for Managing Colonies:

Supervising breeding operations, preserving ideal breeding circumstances, and controlling population dynamics are all part of running a betta fish breeding colony. The following are some methods of colony management to think about:

1. **Breeding Rotation:** To avoid overbreeding, lessen the effects of inbreeding depression, and preserve genetic variety within the colony, rotate breeding couples on a regular basis. Give breeding couples a break in between spawning cycles so they can recover and refuel.

2. **Certifice Matching:** By carefully matching breeding pairings according to certain features, qualities, or interesting genetic markers, you may practice selective pairing. To increase breeding success and provide information for future breeding choices, keep thorough records of all breeding results, fry quality, and genetic features.

3. **Selection:** To preserve breeding quality and eliminate subpar or genetically flawed fry from the breeding population, use culling techniques. Cull fry that exhibit abnormalities, health problems, or unattractive features in order to enhance overall breeding results and stop the spread of genetic illnesses.

4. Rotation of the Tank: Rotate spawning or breeding tanks to maintain the best possible

breeding conditions and avoid the accumulation of pollutants, diseases, or algae. To lower the risk of disease transmission and maintain a healthy breeding environment, clean and disinfect breeding tanks on a regular basis in between breeding cycles.

Sustainability and Genetic Diversity:

A betta fish breeding colony's long-term survival and viability depend on maintaining genetic variety. In addition to boosting hybrid vigor and preventing inbreeding depression, genetic variety also maintains the general resilience and health of the breeding population. In order to encourage genetic variety and sustainability in a betta fish breeding colony, consider the following tactics:

1. **Outcrossing:** Through outcrossing with genetically distant or unrelated individuals, provide fresh genetic material to the breeding colony. The process of outcrossing aids in maintaining genetic diversity within the breeding population as well as expanding the gene pool and introducing novel traits or features.

2. **Testing Genetics:** To determine the genetic heritage and background of breeding animals, do pedigree analysis or genetic testing. To preserve genetic variety and breeding quality, use genetic testing to find carriers of recessive characteristics, forecast offspring phenotypes, and make well-informed breeding choices.

3. **Aims for Breeding:** Establish precise breeding objectives and goals that place a

premium on long-term sustainability, genetic variety, and breeding quality. Create a breeding strategy or plan that details the actions required to accomplish your objectives and monitors the progress of your breeding program over time.

4. **Keeping Documents:** To track genetic variety and keep an eye on breeding quality, keep thorough records of breeding activities, genetic features, breeding results, and population dynamics. To assess the effectiveness of breeding couples, spot breeding patterns, and come to well-informed breeding choices, consult breeding records.

Result:

An effective betta fish breeding colony requires meticulous planning, vigilant maintenance, and a commitment to long-term sustainability, genetic variety, and high-quality reproduction. Betta fish hobbyists may establish robust and healthy breeding colonies that provide young that are healthy and of superior quality by choosing appropriate breeding couples, putting colony management strategies into practice, and encouraging genetic variety. We'll look at improving breeding methods, resolving common problems, and boosting breeding success in betta fish breeding operations in the next chapters.

Chapter 13: Resolving Frequently Assigned Problems in Betta Fish Breeding

While it may be a gratifying and demanding activity, breeding betta fish can provide a number of challenges for breeders to overcome. In this chapter, we'll examine typical issues that could come up throughout the breeding process and provide advice and solutions to assist breeders get beyond these obstacles.

*1. Ineffective Attempts at Spawning:**

Failed spawning efforts, in which breeding partners are unable to effectively spawn or generate viable offspring, are a typical problem that breeders may face. Failed spawning efforts may be caused by a variety of things, such as unsuitable breeding partners, unsuitable breeding settings, or underlying health problems.

Solutions for Issues:

- Determine Pair Compatibility: Based on behavior, temperament, and breeding preparedness, determine if two breeding pairs are compatible. Before trying to spawn bettas, make sure that both male and female show spawning characteristics, such as creating bubble nests, engaging in wooing displays, and engaging in mating rituals.

- Optimize Breeding circumstances: To produce the best possible spawning circumstances for betta fish, review and modify breeding parameters such as water temperature, water quality, tank configuration, and environmental enrichment. Sustain consistent water conditions, provide appropriate locations for spawning, and reduce disturbances to promote fruitful spawning behavior.

- Take Into Account Alternative Pairings: If breeding efforts are unsuccessful even after breeding circumstances are optimized, take into account pairing together alternative betta fish with complementing features, attributes, or genetic origins. Try out several breeding pairings to see which ones work better together and promote successful spawning.

2. Fungal or egg-related infections:

Fungal infections or the formation of egg fungus on fertilized eggs are another frequent problem in betta fish rearing. Fungal spores that infect and devour developing embryos are the source of egg fungus, which lowers the survival rates of fry and causes egg mortality. Inadequate cleanliness, fungus contamination, or low water quality may all lead to fungal illnesses.

Solutions for Issues:

- Maintain Optimal Water Quality: Make sure that metrics related to water quality, including pH, temperature, ammonia, nitrite, and nitrate levels, are within limits that are suitable for the breeding of betta fish. To get rid of garbage and keep your water pure, do routine water changes, substrate vacuuming, and filter cleaning.

- Provide Adequate Oxygenation: Use aeration tools like air stones, sponge filters, or surface agitation to raise the breeding tank's oxygenation levels. Sufficient oxygenation facilitates embryo development and fry survival, inhibits the growth of fungi, and prevents the accumulation of organic waste.

- Apply Antifungal Treatments: Give betta fish who have fungal infections or egg fungus antifungal treatments or pharmaceuticals that are designed to treat these conditions. Carefully follow the manufacturer's recommendations and keep an eye out for any evidence of improvement or deterioration in the condition of the afflicted eggs or fries.

3. Fry Predation or Cannibalism:

In betta fish reproduction, cannibalism, also known as fry predation, is a prevalent problem wherein adult bettas or other tank dwellers may feed on weak fry, leading to elevated rates of fry death. Hunger, territorial aggressiveness, or innate habit may all lead to cannibalism, particularly in crowded or stressful situations.

Solutions for Issues:

- Provide Hiding locations: To provide fry security and refuge, make sure the breeding tank has enough hiding locations, visual obstacles, and shaded regions. To reduce fry predation and provide hiding areas, use fake or real plants, spawning mops, floating vegetation, or breeding traps.

- Remove Aggressive animals: To stop fry predation and lessen stress on fragile fry, identify and remove aggressive or predatory animals from the breeding tank. Rearrange tank decorations or separate aggressive fish into separate tanks to break up the territorial tendency and increase fry survival.

- Feed Adults Enough: To avoid violence or cannibalism motivated by starvation, make sure adult bettas are fed enough. To meet the dietary requirements of adult bettas and reduce predatory behavior, provide high-quality commercial foods, live foods, or nutritional supplements on a regular basis.

4. Inadequate Fry Development or Growth:

Breeders of betta fish are often concerned about poor fry growth or development, which may manifest as stunted growth, anomalies in the development process, or sluggish maturity rates. Poor fry development may be caused by a variety of causes, including as insufficient nutrition, unfavorable environmental circumstances, or genetic predispositions.

Solutions for Issues:

- Offer Nutritious food: To assist betta fry's quick growth and development, provide them with a diverse and nutrient-rich food. To provide sufficient nutrition and encourage healthy development, feed fry often, little meals of premium live or powdered foods like microworms, recently hatched brine shrimp, or commercial fry dicts.

- Maintain Stable Environment: Keep an eye on the temperature, water quality, and water parameters to maintain a stable environment in the fry tank. To maintain perfect water conditions and encourage the best possible growth and development of fry, keep the water temperature between 78 and 82°F (25 and 28°C) and do frequent water changes.

- Cull Inferior Fry: To stop the spread of genetic illnesses and enhance overall breeding quality, identify and remove inferior or genetically flawed fry from the breeding population. Eliminate fry that exhibit abnormalities, health problems, or unwanted characteristics in order to encourage the development of healthier, superior progeny.

Result:

The process of breeding betta fish may be difficult yet rewarding, and breeders may run into a number of problems and difficulties. Breeders may increase breeding success rates by diagnosing and solving common issues including poor fry development, cannibalism, fungus in eggs, and unsuccessful spawning attempts. The happiness of successfully producing healthy, lively betta fish colonies may be experienced by betta fish breeders via the optimization of breeding circumstances, provision of sufficient nutrition, and resolution of underlying problems. We'll look at advanced breeding methods, genetic factors, and advice for optimizing breeding success in betta fish breeding operations in the next chapters.

Chapter 14: Optimizing Breeding Outcomes in Programs for Betta Fish Breeding

In order to maximize breeding success, betta fish breeding operations need to combine meticulous management, strategic planning, and attention to detail. This chapter will cover advanced methods and approaches, including as genetic selection, environmental optimization, health management, and fry care, that maximize breeding success.

Genetic Pairing and Selection:

The key to optimizing breeding success in betta fish breeding operations is genetic matching and selection. Breeders may improve the quality and genetic integrity of their breeding stock by carefully choosing mating couples based on desirable features, genetic variety, and breeding goals. The following tactics may be used to maximize breeding success via matching and genetic selection:

- **Explain Breeding Objectives:** Clearly state the intended qualities, traits, and genetic results in addition to the breeding aims and objectives. Create a breeding strategy or plan that details the actions required to accomplish your objectives and serves as a roadmap for breeding choices.

Assess Genetic Features: To find people with desired attributes and genetic variety, evaluate the genetic traits, traits, and ancestry of possible breeding material. When choosing breeding couples, take into account elements like color, finnage, pattern, body conformation, and genetic ancestry.

- **Genetic Diversity in Balance:** By avoiding excessive inbreeding and adding new genetic material by outcrossing or selective pairing, you can maintain genetic variety within the breeding population. In order to preserve genetic variety and lower the risk of genetic illnesses, try to maintain a balanced gene pool.

- **Review Breeding Results:** To monitor the effectiveness of breeding couples and assess their reproductive potential, keep thorough records of the breeding results, fry quality, and genetic features. Utilize breeding data to pinpoint patterns in breeding, productive pairings, and places where the breeding program needs to be strengthened.

2. Enhancement of the Environment:

To maximize breeding success and support betta fish health, fertility, and spawning behavior, the breeding environment must be optimized. Breeders can establish the perfect breeding habitat that promotes effective spawning and fry survival by offering optimum water conditions, appropriate spawning places, and environmental enrichment. The following tactics may be used to improve the breeding environment:

Preserve Consistent Water Conditions: Keep constant water qualities within ideal limits for betta fish reproduction, including temperature, pH, ammonia, nitrite, and nitrate levels. To maintain immaculate water conditions, do routine substrate vacuuming, water changes, and filter maintenance.

- **Offer Appropriate Reproductive Sites:** To promote natural spawning behavior, provide betta fish with appropriate spawning places, such as bubble nests, spawning mops, or plant leaves. To encourage effective spawning and fry survival, provide a spawning-friendly habitat with plenty of hiding places, floating plants, and visual obstacles.

- **Optimize Water Flow:** Modify the breeding tank's water circulation and flow to better resemble the environment and encourage spawning behavior. To gently stir up the water and provide oxygen without stressing either the fry or breeding couples, use air stones, wavemakers, or modest water movement.

- **Improve Environmental Benefits:** To provide betta fish cover, hiding places, and visual stimulation, enhance the breeding habitat with live plants, hardscape components, and natural decorations. Create a realistic environment with caverns, driftwood, boulders, and floating plants to promote stress-reduction and natural activities.

3. Disease Prevention and Health Management:

Ensuring the long-term sustainability of a betta fish breeding program and optimizing breeding success depend heavily on maintaining optimum health and preventing sickness. Breeders may reduce the danger of disease outbreaks and maximize breeding success by putting preventive health management strategies into place, keeping an eye out for symptoms of sickness, and upholding stringent cleanliness standards. The following are some methods for managing your health and preventing disease:

- **New Items Under Quarantine:** Before adding fresh fish, plants, or aquarium supplies to the breeding tank, quarantine them to stop the spread of illness or parasites. Before moving the quarantined individuals to the breeding tank, use a separate quarantine tank with its own filtration system and keep a tight eye out for any symptoms of sickness.

- **Retain Standards for Hygiene:** Keep your aquarium clean and well-maintained to reduce the amount of organic waste, debris, and diseases that accumulate in the breeding tank. To avoid excessive waste buildup, refrain from overfeeding and clean the aquarium's glass, decorations, and filter media on a regular basis using aquarium-safe cleaning supplies.

Assign a Nutritious Diet: To enhance breeding couples' general health, fertility, and success in reproduction, provide them with a healthy and well-balanced diet. For the best possible breeding conditions, provide premium commercial meals, live foods, and nutritional supplements. These will supply vital vitamins, minerals, and nutrients.

Keep an Eye on Water Quality: Regularly check water quality factors including pH, temperature, ammonia, nitrite, and nitrate levels to guarantee ideal circumstances for fish spawning. Regularly change the water and keep the conditions steady to help betta fish become less stressed and more likely to mate.

4. Handling and Growing Fry:

In order to maximize breeding success and guarantee the survival and development of progeny, fry care and raising is essential. Breeders may develop healthy, lively fry and help their breeding program succeed by giving the best possible diet, surroundings, and fry care procedures. The following are some methods for caring for and raising fry:

Assign a Nutritious Diet: To encourage the quick growth and development of betta fry, provide a variety and nutrient-rich food. To provide sufficient nutrition and encourage healthy development, feed small, frequent meals of premium live or powdered foods, such as microworms, recently hatched brine shrimp, or commercial fry feeds.

Preserve a Stable Environment: Keep an eye on the fry tank's temperature, water quality, and water parameters to maintain consistent environmental conditions. To maintain perfect water conditions and encourage the best possible growth and development of fry, keep the water temperature between 78 and 82°F (25 and 28°C) and do frequent water changes.

Reduce Stress: Reduce stress in betta fry by creating a low-stress habitat with plenty of hiding places, visual obstacles, and covered spaces. Steer clear of situations that might stress out your fry and hinder their growth and health, such as crowded tanks, hostile tankmates, or abrupt environmental changes.

- **Cull Inferior Fry:** To stop the spread of genetic illnesses and enhance overall breeding quality, identify and remove inferior or genetically flawed fry from the breeding pool. Eliminate fry that exhibit abnormalities, health problems, or unwanted characteristics in order to encourage the development of healthier, superior progeny.

Result:

Betta fish breeding systems need to use a diverse strategy to maximize breeding success, which includes genetic selection, habitat optimization, health management, and fry care approaches. Breeders of betta fish may improve the caliber, genetic variety, and general effectiveness of their breeding operations by putting cutting-edge tactics and approaches into practice. The next few chapters will cover more ground on subjects like community involvement, sales, and marketing for betta fish rearing.

Chapter 15: Betta Fish Breeders' Marketing and Sales Strategies

Effective marketing and sales strategies are essential for managing a betta fish breeding business. This chapter will examine several marketing approaches, sales channels, and promotional initiatives that betta fish breeders may use to attract clients, boost revenue, and expand their business.

1. Creating Your Personal Brand:

To stand out from the competition and have a recognized presence in the market, your betta fish breeding firm must have a strong brand identity. Your company name, logo, website, social media accounts, and general style all contribute to your brand identity. The following advice may help you create your brand identity:

- **Select a Catchy Company Name:** Choose a distinctive and catchy company name that captures the spirit of your breeding enterprise and appeals to your intended market. Think about including terms like "Betta Haven" or "AquaBetta Breeds" that are associated with betta fish breeding.

- **Create an Expert Logo:** Design a polished logo that conveys your breeding philosophy, principles, and unique selling propositions while graphically representing your company. Your logo should be scalable, eye-catching, and adaptable enough to be used in a variety of marketing materials and platforms.

- **Create a unified visual style:** Make sure that your website, social media accounts, business cards, and promotional items all have the same visual identity. To strengthen your brand identification and provide clients a unified brand experience, use consistent colors, typefaces, and graphics.

- **Write an Engaging Brand Narrative:** Give your audience a reason to connect with your brand narrative as you share your passion, experience, and adventure in betta fish breeding. To set your brand apart and gain clients' confidence, emphasize your devotion to quality, ethical business operations, and breeding philosophy.

2. Establishing a Virtual Identity:

In order to grow your betta fish breeding company's customer base, establish trust, and reach a wider audience in the modern digital era, you must have a strong online presence. The following are some methods for creating an online presence:

- **Build a Reputable Website:** Provide your betta fish breeds, breeding philosophy, prices, and contact details on a polished website. Improve your website's exposure and draw in organic traffic from prospective clients by optimizing it for search engines (SEO).

Make Use of Social Media: Use social media sites like YouTube, Twitter, Facebook, and Instagram to interact with your audience, post information about your breeding program, and display the betta fish breeds that you have available. Post images, videos, breeding advice, and client endorsements often to establish a connection and draw in followers.

Participate in Online Groups: Take part in community forums, online discussion groups, and online forums devoted to betta fish breeding to build relationships with other breeders, exchange information, and advertise your breeding enterprise. Provide insightful commentary, respond to inquiries, and position yourself as a respected resource in the betta fish breeding industry.

Initiate a Vlog or Blog: Write interesting blog entries, articles, or videos on industry developments, care advice, breeding methods, and betta fish breeding. By sharing your knowledge and experiences with your audience, you may inspire and educate them while increasing traffic to your website and social media accounts.

3. Making Use of Online Shopping Sites:

E-commerce platforms provide betta fish breeders the chance to sell their fish online, expand their customer base, and expedite the sales process. The following are some online marketplaces and e-commerce sites where you may sell your betta fish:

Underwater Marketplaces: Use specialist aquatic markets like Aquabid, BettaFish.com, or BettaFishStore.com to list your betta fish for sale. These sites provide a focused audience of prospective consumers and cater only to betta fish aficionados.

All-purpose E-Commerce Sites: Sell additional aquatic supplies, accessories, or items in addition to your betta fish by using general e-commerce sites like eBay, Etsy, or Amazon. These platforms have the potential to attract clients interested in betta fish and other aquatic items because of their wider audience reach.

- **Your Personal Onlinc Store:** If you want to offer your betta fish to consumers directly, think about creating your own e-commerce website with an integrated online shop. This gives you complete control over the sales process, relationships with customers, branding, and the ability to gradually develop a devoted clientele.

4. Marketing Techniques:

When it comes to drawing clients, boosting revenue, and building brand recognition for your betta fish breeding company, promotional tactics are essential. The following are some advertising tactics to think about:

- **Provide Deals and Promotions:** Offer specials, discounts, or promotions on certain betta fish breeds or breeding pairs to encourage sales and draw in new clients. To generate urgency and promote impulsive purchases, consider offering seasonal promotions, holiday specials, or temporary discounts.

- **Organize Giveaways or Contests:** Run freebies, competitions, or sweepstakes on your website or social media accounts to interact with your audience, build brand awareness, and draw in new fans. Provide betta fish-related goods, rewards, or breeding equipment to encourage involvement and create excitement.

Work together with influencers: Join together with YouTubers, bloggers, or influencers in the betta fish community to expand your brand and attract more customers. Work together on sponsored articles, product reviews, or giveaways to take advantage of their credentials and readership while promoting your company.

Participate in Expos and Events: Take part in aquatic activities, exhibits, and betta fish shows to promote your betta fish breeds, make connections with other enthusiasts, and meet possible clients. Put up a stand, show off your fish in breeding tanks, and interact with guests by giving talks, demonstrations, or handouts.

Result:

Promoting your betta fish breeding company, drawing clients, and increasing sales all depend on your marketing and sales tactics. The market exposure, reach, and profitability of betta fish breeders may be optimized via the implementation of promotional techniques, e-commerce platform use, strong brand identity development, and online presence construction. We'll cover more ground in the next chapters on subjects including future trends in betta fish breeding, sustainability techniques, and customer service.

Printed in Great Britain
by Amazon